YEAR OF THE MURDER HORNET

YEAR OF THE MURDER HORNET

Tina Cane

velizbooks.com

Year of the Murder Hornet © 2022 by Tina Cane

Veliz Books' titles are available to the trade through our website and also our primary distributor, Small Press Distribution (800) 869-7553.
For personal orders, catalogs, or other information, write to
info@velizbooks.com

For further information write Veliz Books: ·
P.O. Box 961273, El Paso, TX 79996, USA
velizbooks.com

ISBN: 978-1-949776-12-6

Cover image by Cormac Crump
Cover design by Silvana Ayala

Printed in the U.S.A.

My heart rouses
　　　　thinking to bring you news
　　　　　　　of something
that concerns you
　　　　and concerns many men. Look at
　　　　　　　　what passes for the new.
You will not find it there but in
　　　　despised poems.

　　　　　　　　—William Carlos Williams, "Asophodel"

Some conversations are not about what they're about.

　　　　　　　　—Anne Carson

I do get that the I on the page is still not me. I do get that.
I don't know if you get that.

　　　　　　　　—Sheila Maldonado, "Temporary Statement"

TABLE OF CONTENTS

I.

II.

III.

I

YEAR OF THE MURDER HORNET

year of the cloud of pollen   that chased me to my car   across the supermarket parking lot

year I was overpowered   by flowering magnolia petals   in a windstorm while walking home

year of the murder hornet   and coronavirus   and weather as a system   that shaped each day

in a way that felt   different from the past   year during which you understood   how the neighborhood

you grew up in   shaped the way you say *friend*   how the word *childhood*   is the start of a sentence

that has no end   until you aren't the one saying it anymore   year of grown-ups   with their gravity

making everything   a question or a fragment   depending on their personal weather   whether

some of them   were green or deep   as trees of your imagining   year when the way trees speak

with each other about each other   was more essential   than the shade they gave   year to try to live

like trees   upright yielding seeking   sunlight and silent languages   year I got a book in the mail

about housecleaning   as a joke from another poet   regarding a poem of mine   about life being hard

and people's constant quest   on the internet   to make things easier   year the cover of the book

read   *Introducing Your Household Heroes: Regular Products with Multiple Abilities*   how *multiple abilities*

sounded more like an affliction   than a capacity   year of nights I lost sleep   year my mind cradled me

GRAMMAR

This morning I woke up
                          wondering if

I had ever really seen   *The Rules of the Game*

or just the poster in a window   twenty-five years ago

on Boulevard Saint Michel
                              sometimes suggestion is enough

when it comes to memory   or anything really   most days

my mind is a sieve   punch drunk from patch work

conjecture   about my place in the world   blah blah blah

I've been alive for decades   but I'm still unsure

whether gravity   travels like electricity   or if it occurs

like a *coup de foudre*
                          stung by both

I've been parsing the grammar   ever since

      am I   *was I*   *subject / object*

      actor or acted upon

so many conditionals   I wish I knew

how *past tense*   meets *perfect aspect*

to make the *perfect past*
                          maybe

you're tense like me   about politics and poetry

love and stimulus   motherhood and pathogens

by tense I mean taut   by taut I mean ready

to diagram anything   that comes my way

I say *ready*   but what I really mean   is willing

ESSAY ON GENTRIFICATION

Gentrification   means I have arrived   in a manner   only half foreseen

as half of me   claims culprit or lays claim   to my neighborhoods and stoops

spanning shambles   to the ramblings of my education
                                        meaning I know

all about espresso   and the benefits of self-expression   meaning I still

trip myself up   as reflex to tradition   for a long line of providing comfort

constitutes survival   prior to mine   if property is still

an interest to protect   it also interests me   in other ways
                                        meaning I spend

my days sweeping the floor   sometimes writing   sometimes imagining a table

strewn with pheasant and clattering plates   where a feast takes place   in my absence

where plans   for re-paving move forward   without my input   or my permission

as I envision the wave of a hand   prompting someone   to pass the bread

to someone who likes   their wine cool   their butter soft and lightly salted

someone akin to me   who warms each pat   with her breath   a hint
                                        of bitter ancestors on it

ESSAY ON POETICS OR EARLY MORNING TEXTING WITH ORLANDO

I'm having trouble writing
                              poetry he wrote trouble being a poetry writer

I don't know I said write notes of sound notes of mystery see what comes

geese flying brakes screeching boots crunching snow on a path I said Do you

recall the last time the light of shadow reflected off your skin? he asked

in the morning I said stretching in bed lowlight we exist he wrote because of light

as light he said sound is light's cousin I replied shadow has a sound of whispering

shadows vibrate like voices he wrote like bird bones are hollow btw I said sound

like wind I added wind moving he wrote against the fabric of skin feeling wind

the epitome of being in the moment we agreed breath is wind   we said write it down

I said see what the shadow gives our breath imitates wind he wrote the crux of it

us as wind   messages in our ears long before the ringing messages of purpose

he said mystery of purpose I noted humility of purpose or mystery fabric of soul

he wrote hella aura yours he said lol poetics of geography and self shadow of words

on the page I typed in person he said insomnia I said sorry
                                                            oh well we said soon

TREATISE ON MY MOUTH

Turns out I am   *chargé d'affaires*

of my own mouth   of my real speech

though I sometimes think   I am just being

emotionally concise   that my use

of constraint   is not about   protecting

my own interests   but instead   implies poetry

but we'll let your mouth

be the judge

of that   I am sure there's a test   or an app

I should probably   ask my kids   for whom my policy

is to never be

alarmist

but rather to appear   as a witness to our lives

so that I can tell them   what they were like

when they were little

to be a regular channel

of love   is my intention   for I am here   to avoid

conflict   while propagating   an accurate narrative

by means   of my one and only mouth   open for business

worthy of attention
                    I am ready

to answer   all of your questions

SHELTER IN PLACE

Schools are shuttered   everything is canceled   and my body has become

an extension of my house   this shift is strange   but not entirely unfamiliar

the way a cardinal's home   is a *disordered stick bomb*   just about captures

how I feel
           how the mother bird uses her shape   as a template to form her nest

shoving sticks together   in a fit of random engineering   *randoming* would be

the verb I guess   or *jamming* as it applies to me
           a steady state of *hysteresis*

in which applied pressure   changes the ensemble   in which the structure

bounces back   but not completely
           I've been thinking

of ways to speak   to my children about fear   how to be adaptive

I want to tell them   about zebra finches   who are content in captivity

and who unlike robins   which favor mud as cement   make their nests

from anything they find   strips of paper or string   fibers from a coconut husk

I want to stress   that these elements the finches assemble   seem haphazardly

placed but behave collectively   how there's a logic buried   deep in the mother

building her nest   which is a story of the nature of her body   as every child's

first home   that we don't struggle alone   as the architects of our days

that nature will continue   to amaze us   in ways we don't expect

ESSAY ON COMFORT OR OPEN LETTER TO SEAN HANNITY

Let not your heart be troubled   Sean Hannity tells his viewers   at the close of each show

possibly the worst   cosmic joke on Earth   plus *trouble* is a relative term   but with poetry

and a pandemic   and art being shared at a distance   we should despair over the state

of the universe   the limits of verse

                           Eliot said *April is the cruelest month*

Ruefle wrote that Anderson wrote   *the secret of poetry is cruelty*   which gets me thinking

about life as a merciless sonnet   my breath at night   iambic in the darkness   where my mind

with its drift of meaningless lists   reels troubled as my heart   while I wait

for the volta   to reveal the true concerns of my existence

                                    I want to break things

or make a break   and seam the cracks with gold   as if scars will make the whole

all the more intriguing

                how a husk holds

the form of what once filled it   how if we really look   we can see

that everything adapts   and everyone is apt   to find comfort where they can

              Dear Sean

              Please go away and never come back.

              All the best,

              Tina

CORONA POEM

Vigilance means crocuses   pushing up in grass   beyond the confines of my home

where hushed tones   and intimations of apocalypse   pervade our every gesture

and everything suddenly exists   as a finite form of future trash

                                              still I remain

devoted to it all   attached to little   more than bread   crystalline from the freezer

for safe-keeping   a new set of coveted staples   includes fresh air   and the scent

of my daughter's head   wet from the shower   the way she says Yes   as she unveils

her mane freshly chopped   in a fit of boredom   two thick braids still in their elastics

curved like parentheses on her desk

                            another Yes   as known systems

dismantle within days   I meant to compose a tone poem   here today

thinking how another poet wrote   *I can only be myself when my household is asleep*

how now nothing keeps me awake more   than the notion   that it will all go away

BLUE

Blue is the mind   in a state of *focused immediacy*   blue is water

working against the body   so it can get there

then there's the sky

in September   open and azure as America   least American Dream-*iest* of lands

on the face of the planet   where like most   I hoard the future and try not

to be afraid   that a snag in the food chain   will stop the *Steak-Umm's* corporation

from dispensing its daily wisdom via twitter

by *food* I mean *supply*

by *supply* I mean   I've had enough   inadvertent exposure

to *quarantine baking fails*   and *celebrities sheltering-in*   to last at least

the time it takes   for grief to finds its way   back home which I know

from experience   is not as long   or brief as you might think

when's the last time

you heard a child describe the silence

in a room as the sound   of someone crying   I couldn't tell you

these days are indistinct   but it happened

recently one friend said

Time no longer has meaning   *Today I cleaned* my oven   *Wow* I said

It really doesn't   Wow

ESSAY ON THE ADVANCEMENT OF TIME

My imaginary allegiance
                        to the *Anti-Nostalgia*

Association for the Advancement of Time   is partly a reaction

to Proust   inspired and ambivalent   as my response to the wall

of moms in Portland   one rumored note of hope   amid all those trees

swaying in solidarity   with the leaf-blowing dads   earnest home-grown

protectors of women's bodies
                        ever the bulwark against

everything   women's bodies I mean   even in war somehow

even against the self somehow   but   how can I not be moved

you ask   by a person's willingness   to put their body

on the line   when I hardly know   what to do with mine

half the time
                        I'm slouching or speaking loudly

using words that convey too much nuance   it's hard

I try not to judge   but love   is a process of education

like the Greeks said   which is what   this poem is about   love

as a way to reciprocate   our imperfections   not bend in service

to a lie   about life
                        the way women's

bodies can sway   carries each day

into night   the heaviest of weight made light

DESIGNATED NEW YORKER

It is my heart
                    I mean my heart   back in New York

that nature's breaking   the way a mother breaks   for what

she cannot leave
                    once upon a time

the city was a pillar to me   third leg of my proverbial stool

the other two being   weed and the street   meaning my heart

can be scarred   or slow to forgive   meaning it knows

that towers fall   that pillars falter
                                    but faithful still

I walk myself each day   like I'm my own dog   sole owner

of my animal fears   in need of peace and fresh air   like children

and linens   like the wind   which in French is *le vent*

root of ventilator   wind-maker   to lift the sails

of ailing lungs   in Elmhurst, Queens and beyond

to stir the souls   beneath the hallowed ground

we now call Freedom
                    it is my heart

I mean my heart   back in New York

that breaks as it designates   love for firefighters   especially those who scaled the smoky stairs   who carried the living and the dead

in their arms   who carry them still
                                        love also

from afar   for truckers and clerks and nurses   for my mail carrier Mike

and women around the world   who march for their rights

while men throw rocks at them   and when there's no more stones

they throw their shoes
                        love too

for dolphins who   fake news   never once swam

in the canals of Venice   but love nonetheless for all

the stories   too thrilling to be true
                                        love even

for molecules   that might kill me   in the subway

of my mind   or from across the six-foot divide   at the check-out line

and for wintergreen mints   tossed in my basket   at the last second

their hospital scent   suddenly synonymous   with death

and pandemic
                    it is my heart

I mean relentless   resident of love   that grows to a towering proportion

in the absence of those   who were stolen   or who slipped away

it is my heart   which counts you and me   among those   who get to stay

REGIME

eat a diet of night shades   reverse climate change

avert colony collapse disorder   defuse a bomb disguised as love

stew tomatoes for deep sleep   and blood that's mineral rich

with new mysteries   pump that blood   like a fever dream

through your bittersweet heart   and wait for your mind

to fortify against   petulant businessmen   celebrities

with special pajamas   the peach-colored women

of Instagram   be wary of optimists with Keto tips

and people who seek to be president   munch a plate of jalapeños

and jimson weed   listen to those   in love with curiosity

the moon and her many moods   stay tuned to souls

that brood and to poets   who like finches in cages

sense the changes   before they come

EMPIRE

History's always showing me   men on boats   and women in houses

but *memory is a poet   not an historian*   and I must be victor

of my own mind   to tell my stories   of conquest and demise

in which the soft fascination   of watching waves   while parsing marriage

is a movement   towards perspective   that still falls short

of a bolder effort
                    like a mother

naming her son   *I am Empire*   with no hint of irony at all

I confess
                to a relative lack of courage   as I put my intentions

down on paper   put the paper in a bucket   and let the paper

burn in my head   fire mixed with thoughts   mixed with words

so many variants of concern
                        and still no memory

worth preserving   more than the sight   of my first-born son

flipping his skateboard   on a curb in New York

the whole history   of his body in the world

DISPOSABLE MASK

like the broken wing of a blue jay   the color of a robin's egg   and today

my youngest son wept   inexplicable tears   his body limp   with the million

things he's seen and heard   in his ten years
                                            these past few months

his sister assures me   he understands everything   just doesn't have the words

but I am not assured   I can feel all the languages   pulsing at his temple

beneath my lips   I kiss his hot skin   press my cheek too hard against his

trying to absorb   every last bit of hurt from him   to take on his sadness

and mask my own   having mistook   a swatch of fabric   stuck in a tree

for a swath of sky   so eager to find   a sign of the advent

of spring   to shepherd him back   towards simpler things

HOLD

Sometimes   it's a shock event   in lieu of a total coup

an instance more akin   to the slow overthrow   of familiar systems

how the course of a day   lapses into years
                           then breaks

I used to say   *The day is long*   Seasons pass   back when Samantha

would have her toddlers in pajamas   by four-thirty in the afternoon   *It's dark out*

They don't know   she'd laugh and I'd laugh
                         across the phone line

which could have been a sea   for how vast the distance felt   treading February

as we were   newer versions of our selves   we ourselves hardly even knew

and now Nicole
              has cancer

yet appears more radiant than ever   as if lit from within   by the threat of death

she projects   such a fierce desire to live   I want to tell everyone   about her

poems which she reads   on the internet   from her bed
                    which stun me

for the clarity   I force upon myself   by witnessing them

in the dark   as my family sleeps   phone aglow in my palm

shock of birds

shock of scans

shock of nodes

shock of breast-

less woman kind

                    at the end Nicole

always places her hand   flat on the screen   as if pressing it

against mine   not to say *Stop*   or to dispute my meaning

but to hold me   in the feeling of her thought

JOY IN REPETITION

Joy in repetition he wrote   because everything is Prince   and we wept

separately   via email   because the words were falling all over themselves

and worlds were falling down   we were getting older   but somehow

younger too   and there was magic and sex   and apple pie in the mouth   every

guitar solo was like water   and water was everywhere   the invention of water

coming from where   solid ground gives way   cut the poetics bullshit

we agreed   enough of Bloomingdale's

                                       meet me at the beautiful bodega

I'll be in blue   crushing it with my backpack   of synaptic love and mystery

IDEAS

The ache   of being in love   with an idea

makes my life   make sense somehow   like how

the final scene in *The 400 Blows*   leaves me feeling grief-

stricken yet invincible
                    the way my father said *Fight, Fight*

when he realized he was dying   his voice so faint   I had to ask

the resident   on the phone to translate   the man's young voice

broke as he said the words
                        I told the doctors

they couldn't let my father go   until I got there   until he said so

impractical until the end   my dad held on
                                    just long enough

for me to comprehend   my adoration of him   for me to read Whitman

to his alive unconscious   in the hospital bed

as he came to grips with
                    what his fingers

on the blanket   kept reaching to grasp   I guess

or was it my hand   the idea of my hand

OF ALL THINGS

Of all things   the Dead Sea is dying   and here I am   I still have hands

with which to work and live   and every day I believe   I can become

something different   most days I walk the woods   ready for the green-

lucid vibrations   of all things   to find me   as I think and move

past saplings   without killing them
                    I know all things

must die in their own time   so I keep my hands to myself

leaving only   with what I brought   adding only   this delicate dispatch

to the images I store   of evergreen California   or Ashbery's

chorus of trees
             a stash of small prayers

and promises   I make to myself   about potentiality

like one day   I'll see the Redwoods   of all things   like one day

I'll write a book   about lived experience   and the power of expression

about experience   as an expression of power   or power as expressed

potential
        in the interim

I hoard my authority   of all things   the way a library   stores knowledge

which untapped   as sap beneath bark   exists all the same   so yes

like me a tree   needs no witness   to prove its existence
                                        but whatever

the question   I will always answer   *It is what it is*   if you ask

why do I begin with death   of all things   here with the dying sea

I'd say it also has to do   with a postcard Mary sent me   of a sketch

her husband did
                a nihilist hopscotch grid   of all things

words like   *if only*   HAVE TOS   *don'ts   nos   can'ts*   written

in the little squares   which reminded me of what   Sean said

about my poem   not being ready
                            or was it   the poet?

on *Strathmore Imperial Cold Press*   Mary wrote   *I thought you*

whereas   I thought *No*   but also *Yes*
                            then stepping outside

myself   I took a photo of puffy white clouds   of all things   against a flat blue sky

So it goes   I wrote on the caption line   meaning the world moves on   despite

our myriad grievances   meaning movement hurts   whereas clouds

weigh a million pounds   and make magnificence look easy
                                    movement hurts

is also how   I described a police cruiser   of all things   consumed by flames

back in summer   when the world was a ball of pain   and even *time off*

felt burdensome   the world burdened as it was   what it is
                                    pattern and practice

innocuous as wishbones   of all things   I pluck from chickens   boil clean

and place along the sill   in my kitchen   who notices I wonder

the trivial   otherness of others   besides psychologists and poets

it takes courage   to be a person   most of the time
                                                                                                pattern and practice

universal as cruelty   of all things   simple as apple pie   one man saying

I wear your scorn with pride   while another man tells   *America,*

I'm proud to deserve to die
                                                O tired overtures

of equivalency   if context is everything   let's admit

only trees   of all things   are truly honest   the way they display

their seasons so nakedly   while stars in the sky   keep emitting their light

even long after they've died   of all things
                                                                                night

grips me   with its cluster of yearning and concerns   in the lowlight

of a ghost dream   I learn to love my concerns   of all things

yearn to lavish them   like a slaughter of lovers
                                                                                I've been using

the word *attendant* a lot   not from the French   act of waiting

but meaning   *related or connected to*   matters of the heart

and mind   as in   a constellation of attendant issues   but I find if I stop thinking   and just feel   it really is   about the waiting

          sunlight   and its *attendant* warmth

          findings   and their *attendant* fallout

          fall   and its *attendant* leaflessness

and Jesus   of all things   turns out   is also all about
the waiting   plus mystery

                rising   rising   risen

what with Easter come and gone   this year was just   one long metaphor

Who is anyone   without the people   they love?   my son scrawled

on a sheet of stray loose leaf

                maybe I'm in it   for the fragments

of all things   *Shallow convictions   Uncertain substance*

words my dad wrote   in a speckled notebook   I found beneath his bed

after his death   fragments

              Mozart   Mendelssohn   Puccini

              Haydn   Symphony #51

thoughts about Gatsby   of all things   who is anyone?

Cheyenne Diner, 33th & 9th   Meatball Parm $2.75   a dozen

pit stops in Hell's Kitchen

             I say *father* here

when I should say *fathers*   since there were others   I never even knew

the first one was Caucasian   and fought in Vietnam   which meant they

didn't make him   play the Viet Cong   of all things   during war games at Fort Dix

like they did that Chinese man   who was not my father either

                                                    but still

he returned unspared   after two tours   sat speechless in a chair   unable

to form words   around memories   of all things   or the people he loved

or my other dad

                     the one with the notebook   born in the county of Kings

near the Bay of Sheep   in the middle of the woods   of all things   if the woods

had looked like the street   across from Ebbets Field   where he spent his boyhood

praying for balls to clear the wall   so he could take one home   to put under his pillow

with his radio   tuned to the game

                           maybe I'm in it

for the mystery   of all things   fragments of me   Anatolian or Greek

another father's strands   intertwined with mine   imagined

inheritance   inscrutable as a crest of no lineage   useless

as all my ancient armor   as science   in the face of faith

I say *fathers*   but when the definition   has to do with presence

I say *father   who art in heaven*   by which I mean nothing

but the singular   propulsion of my beloved poetries

                           maybe I mean

my darkest teenage reveries   of all things   caught between graffitied cars

on the D train   maybe that's what   I'm in it for   how smoking

or holding my breath   felt the same   as I clutched the rattling

chains for balance   of all things   entering each station

from the darkened tunnels was like   day breaking every 4 minutes

some squalid revelation   in the time it took   to finish a cigarette

my palms   sometimes smelling of smoke and metal

of all things   metal always smelling like blood

COME CORRECT

Continue to verb   Orlando urges me   via early morning text

I'm trying I write back   *Continue to create* he says   as I get out of bed

raise the window shade
                              distance means   the end of snow days

so I make a dozen snowballs   and keep them in the freezer   after lunch

I give my son   a stone to tumble   in his pocket   for when we walk the woods

I call it his thinking stone   instead of the worrying kind   your thoughts are your own

I tell him   as are mine
                         Pray here, you can ask for anything

whisper the trees   but I have only enough   reverence for words

looking down I see   I'm knee-deep in leaves   it's hard to make out

where the yellows begin   the ambers end
                                        I want

to teach my kids   to come correct   but such words stick

thick and metallic between my lips   when I move to form them
                                              These tongues

full of nostalgia   my young student writes   *I love them*   *I have not loved*   *being so alone*

Sometimes a notebook   I tell him   *is just a notebook*   sometimes love is a butterfly

being crushed by a car
                         it troubles me

that worry can be a form of prayer   as if losing sleep   is a type of pleading

pleading a kind of church
                                        but I don't pray

and try not to worry much

HEARSAY

I'm here I say   but you hear

something else   I am saying

something else   here

POEM BY A PERSON CALLED WOMAN

Ancient as math   bright as grass   I believe in rain

as much as the next person called poet   as much as people

called women   in North Korea   trimming meadows with scissors

blade by blade
                    Not Today, Satan   proclaims the First Baptist

Church on North Main
                              but it *is* Satan's day   and that's not

me being pessimistic   that's the sexy Handmaid Halloween

costume talking   *Vichy France with tits*   double-agent

of the patriarchy Kim Kardashian   and her husband with his MAGA hat

on the verge of mental collapse   or world domination
                                                    that's Orlando

not the tragedy of pulse   but the Native tragedy   of my friend's history

and his early morning texts   calling my coffee   which I have yet to drink

colonial and shit   a forced luxury like flour and bacon   *I hear you* I say

I have to make my kids colonial pancakes   today   *we don't exist*

at all he says   *we will always die and die*   ain't I a woman

I want to know   *Yeah* says Orlando   *you're my homie*

JANUARY EXCEPTION

One article of my personal constitution   is the *January exception*

which I interpret as a question   of freedom and release   how emptiness

enhances opulence   the way a warehouse   further dignifies a Rembrandt

Miles Davis said   *Play what's not there*

                                    so I'm trying

to tell the stories that matter   but I mostly only know   what matters

most to me   maybe real   is what I mean   not to be confused with true

maybe I mean   *anti-matter*   a cancelling-out

                                            I heard the term

hygiene theater   the other day   being used to describe

the performance of safety   as in a shower curtain

hung between cashiers   which made me think of silence

between lovers   but the kind that is different   from intimacy

this morning

                  my son showed me   the photo of a presence

someone glimpsed   within the strobe   atop the Freedom Tower

Was it God? An angel? A holy cross?   the comments section

on the internet lit up   like a mini mega church   my son said

one person wrote

                  "I love you, Jesus. I'll do better"

we cracked up but agreed   it was a worthy sentiment

though the guilt part   was a little sad
                                                  we were waiting

for the light to change   when my son asked   *What do you think is*

a human's purpose on Earth?   That's the big question, isn't it? I said

Or is it? he mused   feigning mystery   with a furrowed brow

just then an ambulance   went blaring past   its sirens

drowned out all thought
                                          I keep feeling

everything's gone to hell   since David Bowie died   for a time

my tendency to doom-scroll   was a nervous tic   until I snapped

myself out of it
                          through a deliberate practice

of remembering   I remember   my dad once told me

"Don't pick up someone else's tab"   I had been a waitress

for so long   I often conflated the service industry   with other

parts of me   like my emotional life
                                                      yesterday

my son came downstairs   in his bedhead and plaid pajamas   talking

about *The Great Conjunction*   which happens when Jupiter and Saturn

travel together across the sky   *That's the Universe for you* I replied

I will be thirty when that happens again   he sighed   *And what*

a wonderful man you will be   I smiled
                                                        what a world

where Mercury is currently in retrograde   where my son was born

Capricorn and I Gemini   meant to be Virgo
                                                        I arrived

so early   they made my mother choose   whose life to save

she chose mine   and later made me   an orphan in other ways

to admit
                  one's own story is the toughest part   I came out

small enough to be swaddled   in a handkerchief   compact

as a cornish hen   housed in a bell jar   with a pump for lungs

I sometimes open my palm   put a clementine in it   to delight my children

by showing them   just how very tiny
                                                        meanwhile

It's like woke meeting up in here   I text Tongo

what Chapelle said   and we laugh from different coasts   like I'll meet you

half-way   because that ocean is vast   and *I know all the fraglities*   we're joking

but we're also   crying jagged tears   brittle resistances   patched with words

like gold
                  the way *kintsugi* mends a bowl   with a gold line along the seam

like the line   I used to want between my teeth   like I was street

which I was   but streets vary you know
                                                        sometimes

I make myself laugh   because I am a poet   no exception

and with February afoot   I need people now

ESSAY ON MOVEMENT

There's a writer
                    I like her mind

how she jotted   *Walk/Adventure!*   on a slip of paper for her daughter   while they were confined

to their apartment in New York City   *It was good to keep possibility alive* she wrote   I took note

since she and I are both   mothers/writers   she was sick at the time with coronavirus   while I

was just suffering   from fatalism and being far from home   my heart broke   almost daily and more

for the shuttered stores and filthy delis   the souls being tallied at a distance   beneath white tents

in Central Park
                    Walk/Adventure!

has always been my ethos   I spent half my life walking it off   across the Village

Chinatown and Soho   the Lower East Side   I might have practiced radical acceptance

had I known   what it was back then
                                        it's not easy   picturing the writer I like   alone

feverish and huddled in damp bedclothes   her essay on a laptop   while her daughter

in diapers crawls on the carpet
                                it's not easy   hearing my own daughter

describe the day   the virus shut her school   as frantic but slow   like a fever dream

the way she and her friends   hurried to empty their lockers   into borrowed paper bags

before rushing to the bus   their arms loaded up with books   how she was the only one

who didn't seem sad or cry   she said all she felt was freedom   and she didn't know why

ESSAY ON STATES

The ambient kind   like surroundings   or like jazz

Coltrane   the heart's improvisation   meaning crying

as a form of music   joy of delectable blues   every organ a body

with its own aria   whether reverence or *arrivederci*
                        states vary

depending on conditions in space   time has to do   with how you move through it

in life my dad said   mine was a trial by fire   *The whole thing?* I exclaimed

I don't know he said   shaking his head   as I watched my form enter

a room full of flames
                How does the end of the universe make you feel?

a cosmologist on the radio   was asking her colleagues   as I merged

into a lane of cars   *Impossible!*   I shouted

three out of four vehicles   the exact same model and make   it turns out

the cosmologist's colleagues   had mixed feelings   about the end of things

like any of us
          the laws of physics

were purportedly different   early on   back when things

were in a denser state   and everything was like love

or a black hole   a black hole being a zone   where light can't escape

love being a time and space   outside of place

GOING THROUGH SOME THINGS

I was going through   some things
                                    a cache of love letters

old impulse control paperwork   gum wrappers and a mint

that tasted like keys
                        I was wearing my flavor-blasted glasses

and gazing at the skyline   aflame in defiance

of nightfall
              I was recalling

the fact that ash   makes the most glorious sunsets   something I once read

in a science journal   in the waiting room at the dentist   a piece of information

so ephemeral and alive with possibility
                                it corresponded

with my subconscious   primordial and sweet

as American crude
                but I wasn't in the mood

to go that deep   if only to keep grief at bay   sometimes we say

what we say   because the Earth is giving up on us   and we know it

sometimes I say   what I say   because I'm not ready to give in

WHAT WE TALK ABOUT WHEN WE TALK ABOUT PATHS:
A Narrative in Captions

Path Today: Fresh Path: Another Kind of Path: Current Path: High School Path: Path of Discernment: Public Speaking Path: Path to the Podium: Monday Morning Path: Path of Least Resistance: Back at It: Path: Sometimes a Path Is a Maze: Another Kind of Path Is Writing: Water Finds a Path: Self-Guided Path: Roberta Flack Is Also a Path: Sometimes It's a Path Across Clouds: Self-Guided Path Through Water:

A Present Path Reflects the Future and the Past: Some Paths Are Hard: Swimming Is Sex and Death

and Thinking and These Things Mean the World to Me So Don't Let My Heart Be Brief Let Me Stick

with This Vision: Path of Grass: Water With Its Perfect Memory Holds My Nostalgia Without Weight:

Sometimes Paths Cross: Path to Nowhere: Some Days I Can't Find a Friggin' Path: Path of My (Resis)

(Exis)tence: I-Can-Walk-and-Chew-Gum-at-the-Same-Time-Just-Saying Path: Fireproof Path: Path of My

Persistence: Hotel/Motel: New Hotel: Death Star: Path to My Panel: Path Home: Find a Path That Feeds You:

Some Sun: Rothko Is a Path: The S.O.S. Band / That's All: Path of Self-Preservation: Apparatus Is a Path:

Path to CVS: Where My Coupons at?: Where Harmony Meets Pleasant / For Real: Snack Path: Not Clementines

But Also Good: Red Path: Sym(path)y: Tele(path)y: Or Narcolepsy: Em(path)y: Path(os): Hydro(path)y

Is a Thing: Cake: Not an Obvious Path: Blue Blue Electric Blue That's the Color of My Room: Two Cakes:

Cake Is Where You Find It: Cake upon Cake upon Cake: Cake: Up: Close Cake: Up Closer: Icing Isn't

Everything: Icing up Close: Most American Cake: Handwork: The Rough Heart of a Grassy-Eyed Rose:

Kindred Spirit to the Tree: Crush: Crush(ed): Crush(able): Cold Crush: (Orange) Crush of Nostalgia:

Crush Groove: Crush(ingly): What Justifies My Hunger for Other Ways of Life Hasn't America Been

Mostly Good (Enough) to Me Like the 80s Like Boy-friends Like Luck: C(rush) or Deep Sleep(er): Crush:

The One Living Poem I've Made: Crush: As When Two Shores Refuse to Touch as When Lapsed Love

Is as Much Distance as Diffidence: Back at It: Sunday Sunday: Track Jacket with Flat Tire Plus Grimace:

A Pastoral: Evelyn "Champagne" King / That's All: Path of Light or Friendly Poltergeist: Need a New Tire:

Tired of Driving: Plus Grimace: An Anti-Pastoral: No Cake: Still Driving on a Spare: Plus Roadside Construction:

There's a Metaphor in There: Just Jamming to Chic in My Kitchen Pregnant Again but Don't Judge the 80s Were

Good to Me in Their Way: Path Towards Clouds or The Ridge = No More Scrambling on All Fours: Kids

on a Ledge or What, Mom?: Done: Road to Galilee: Ready: Terrible Music or Beautiful Fireworks or America

the Terrible/Beautiful: Sundial or Something Simple: Alma's Hand Is Its Own Eclipse or Actual Rainbow

Around the Sun: Fog Obscured by Sunset or Someone's Lonely Light: What's with the Creepy Hello?

or Sleepy Beachside Tradition: La Jetée or Morning at Point Judith: Liquid Summer or Hey, Mom Look:

Kids on Rocks: Kids on Rocks V.20: New (Used) Track Jacket or My Strange Collection: Path to Spiderman:

Big Wheel Keeps on Turning or My Shaky Hand: Titian Back at It: Sea or Sky: At My Desk or Work

Around the Work: Back at It NYC: The Pavement Is Parched or No Amount of Water Will Clean This Street:

I Heart NY: Some Sneakers: Youngest Son: Back at It: Lunchbox: The Terrible Mall or Path to Consumption: Saturday in Brooklyn or It's Been a While: Some Sew by Night: Backpack Treasure or It's the Small Things: Rain, Rain Go Away: Little Titian Forever or Just Back from the Doll Hospital: On the Road with My Oldest or Mobile Office With Skateboard: Schmear: Skaters Eating Bagels & Lox: Of Murray?: All Set with Thompkins

Square or Time for Stromboli: Quick Skate Before the Train: No Skating Allowed or Are You the Mom Here?

Some Citrus or 5h: Homework Folder or Tiny Pencils Are a Thing: "Without Bringing any Other People into

the Planning Loop / I Have Decided to Have Breakfast" or Granola: Epigraph or Exactement: Tough to Choose

Which Piece to Read or Whose Tender Eye? Among the Olive Trees or Dream Retreat: Happy National Daughters

Day or She's Amazing: Back at It or May Need New Shoulders: Jenny Holzer Often Speaks the Truth: Des Phrases:

Many Selves at MASS MoCA: Priming for the Patriarchy or Someone's Idea of a Game Circa 1968: Fun in Their

Hotel Room or The Kind of Thing They Send Me: Board Game Circa 1979 or Maybe Too Soon? or Maybe Never?:

Sky in the Water in the Forest in the Sky: Trying to See or Prospective / Perspective: C'est Tout: Nope: If You Say

So: Someone Turned Thirteen or Back When She Could Channel Gilda Radner: Paths: Apparition in Linoleum

or My Subconscious: Aux Epaules: Table Tennis / Work or Play or How a Somewhat Visual / Verbal Person Has

to Operate / Impractical: Precipice: Progress: Waiting Is the Hardest Part or Window: Concrete Messages: Post-It

or For the Love of God, What Does This Say?: Everything Had a Halo: Night Shift / Purple Crane: "Freak Out in a Moon Age Daydream, Oh Yeah": Eye'(m) Thinking About It All: Supposed Snow Day: Make Your Own

Snow Day: Pretty Presentation of a Path: Back at It: Peluche: Peluche 2 / Il Fait Toujours Froid Là-Bas: About

to Witness the Strength of Street Knowledge: Back at It: Laps: Nature Scribbles: Clearing My Head or The Cake

Called for a lb. of Butter, a lb. of Sugar, a lb. of Coconut and a lb. of Cream Cheese: It Weighed Over 7 lbs.

After We Had Eaten 1/4 of It: Piece de Résistance: Somehow This Exists: Three-Fold Path: Swim to Think:

The Cautionary Part of the Tale: Walk to Think: At the Carwash / Bourbon Scent or I'll Have a Manhattan:

Trying: Trying Again: Someone Turned Ten: Self-Portrait as Sasquatch: Someone Needs a New Board: Sometimes

It Involves Standing Around: As Seen on My Laptop or Working: Saturday = Some Pinball: Working It Out on the Treadmill Again: Back at It: Walk to Think: Social / Emotional Learning or I am Very Relaxed: Shoot Hoops

to Think: Shoot the Moon: Disco Clinic in the Kitchen or Path of Procrastination: Path of Thread: Spider Web

or Nature's Strongest Net: Some Things Change / Some Stay the Same: Night Fever, Night Fever: Conditions:

Back at It: Cheetos: Carrots: Cheetos' Healthy Cousin: or Happy, Now?: Everything Is Going to Be Okay or

Essentials: Current Condition or Small World for the Foreseeable Future: Not My President or Please Get Tested:

Walk to Stay Sane or Sunshine as Disinfectant: Hoops to Stay Sane or Poem-a-Day: Atlantic Avenue Station or

Strange New Subway: T Is for Tina or Trying Hard in Trying Times: Salt Air: Dappled Path or Chugging Along:

Back at It: Hoops or Day 1: Homeschool: More Hoops or Homeschool Day 2: Back at It: Cheetos: Trying to Write or WTF is Happening? Laughing/Crying/Jeez: Dear Swimming Pool, I miss you. Love, Tina. P.S. I Heart NY:

Current Condition: T is for Tina or Trying Hard at "Distance Learning": Hoops at 10:15 or Recess for Distance

Learners: Empire State of Mind: Rainy Day Path: Low-Energy with Biblical Hailstorm: Rainy Walk or Waiting

for a Rainbow: Monday Morning Coffee Break: Snack Attack: So It Goes: (Only) So Much Can Be Solved by

Maniacally Shooting Hoops: "I know to walk myself / like I'm my own dog / sole owner of my animal fears":

LIBRETTO

Every person can look back on their life and see a great opera
—John Giorno

One goal is to choose   astonishment   over nostalgia

the emotional equivalent   of opting for an elegant aunt

over a sad cheap cousin
                              but to be honest

I spend a good part of each day   snared in the soft panic

of reminiscence   at times I feel two steps away   from being

a barfly
              some old guy   lit by the glow   of a Miller High Life sign

stooped over early morning whiskey   as the world outside

mills about buttering their toast
                                        the other night though

I read a poem   that began with a breakfast tray   and a purple martin

bird and which   several lines later   became a letter

to Trayvon Martin
                        it reminded me of a poem

I had written about rinsing rice   that wound up being about

a child named Tamir   I felt connected to the poet   by this similarity of movement   something having to do   with yearning and helplessness

and as I read   from the stack of books   piled on the doll bed

my daughter is no longer interested in   and which I now use as a shelf

I felt compelled to write another poem
                                          about Bucky Dent

the Yankees shortstop   I had a crush on   when I was nine

in my head in the dark   as I wrote my way   toward dreaming

I could hear   1978 all over again   the whole year cracking against

Bucky's bat   a canned but thrilling aria   mixed with fear and death

(NO) REGERTS

no regerts: an unfortunate tattoo that was supposed to be "no regrets."

Each morning I rise   drink deep   from the cup of (no) regerts   a mug that belongs to my son

which I have   taken possession of   whose phrase possesses me   like a philosophy

of the absurd   or a song I've heard   and cannot get out of my head   (no) regerts

that every child became my child   once I became a mother   that the world became   a sharp corner

the intentions of others   a blind corridor   through which to feel my way   (no) regerts   that if I could see

ten steps ahead   even for a stranger's child   I would be clairvoyant   also in my own regard   (no) regerts

for the man at the march   with his Nah, Bro   Miss Rosa Parks, 1955 t-shirt   his smile full of sass

because (no) regerts   about what's right   100% of the time   and (no) regerts   that late at night   I read

instead of doing other   things I should be doing   (no) regerts   I told my first-born son   that the Honorable

Elijah Cummings said   You always have time to do   the things you should be doing   (no) regerts

that my son told me   I was a hypocrite   because karma is a bitch   and I too was a pain in the ass

at 16   (no) regerts   for the luck I tried   time and time again   for the time   I bit my lip until it bled trying not to cry   (no) regerts   what can I say   I liked a boy who rode a skateboard   whose friend held

a gun   to his girlfriend's head   regrets run deep   no one got hurt   but everyone was hurting   (no) regerts

for the chocolate milk I drank   the chips I ate for breakfast   every day for a year   in the dark car

on the D train   (no) regerts   that I waited until now   to really read Proust in French   (no) regerts

that I spent over $600   on a set of books   being shipped from England   this very second   (no) regerts

for lost time or for the fact   that when my mother-in-law   professed to have no regrets   I did not believe her

we get to say   what we want when we are dying   truth is in   the feeling not the facts   the needing to ask

to matter   how people often   only gather round a life once it's gone   (no) regerts   once upon a time

there was a man   who dug his father's grave   (no) regerts   it took him two days   while his sister built

the coffin in their barn   (no) regerts   that I think of this often   in connection with the dirt   I tossed

on my own father's casket   final gesture so scant it hurt   Handfuls mean much   the gravedigger alleged

Okay, but the digging I said   to pay the rent   would make everyone   never want to pay the rent again

(no) regerts   not your money but your life   when I speak of greatness   I mean the basics   plus laughter

and sex and sleep   (no) regerts   that we never were   what we now are   (no) regerts   is how we get this far

UNDER A CLEAN MOON

I'm here with you

and the falling snow

a human unit of meaning

set upon a pillow   a pillow mint

but not as fresh   and burdened

by words   as real

as silence as tears

don't call it here   call it now

now the coup   of unarmed truth

now the people   we've loved

as one   window open   with

the tension of an eclipse

awe of air   awe of theft

all notions become breath

MYSTERIOUS WAYS

I'm imagining Jesus   moving like the moon   through corn fields   wondering

myself into a thicket   and reflecting on the nature of permission   as I read about

John Berryman's letter to his landlord   in which he complains about

his screaming Frigidaire
                    We all have our fridges to bear

the critic quips   and I laugh out loud   in my bed

nestled in amber lamp light   where despite a heavy blanket   I spend the night

tossing and turning   to avoid squashing   my busted shoulder   as if

all hope   were contained in my right rotator cuff   as if the ability to pivot

could be crushed   by intermittent dreams   spinning in half-sleep

I list positions I know:

                    physical   political   sexual

                    my disposition   my orientation   my mission

in this life and next   my mind leaps   to a hospital in Jerusalem

where I heard there's a whole ward   for people who believe they're Jesus

where clothed in white robes   they move through midnight corridors

the walls like grail
                    it's morning now

and I'm hoping to get a letter from Mary   who dispenses wisdom via snail mail

How do you know when something is finished?   people often ask her

When I am done thinking about it   she always says   *But what if the thinking*

never ends? I write back   What then?

ESSAY ON SOUND

Poetry is unfamiliar

these days he wrote   I'm making breakfast for my kids I said

unfamiliar how? I've been on the outside I added   there's no more mystery he replied

dang, what breakfast you making? he wanted to know   yes I said   oatmeal I wrote

and sent an accidental audio clip   of dishes clattering in my sink   oops I said   oops

is better he countered   I like the sound of oops   possibilities there I typed for sure

you didn't make a mistake he wrote back   you just sounded the moment   be the audio

of your moments   sounding the moment   suddenly seems so important I agreed

don't be afraid of sound he told me   it's your identity   in one of my poems I wrote

I have the lines   *the person on the inside / is me / I am the person*   *and also the video*

I haven't thought enough about sound I texted   in relation to the self I added   I think

I am always attaching   meaning to sound   perhaps instead of listening   I would say

he started   *I am the person and also the video* is somewhat interesting   but sonically

in terms of words?   not!   hearing vs. listening vs. feeling was my response   it's not

sonically interesting I typed   I wasn't thinking   about sound or feeling about sound

work the syllables he advised   work the sounds   I like meaning too but don't sacrifice

your sounds for it!   yes I said   French buried in my head tends to help   but I am not always

concerned with sound   not enough maybe   you must be concerned   he insisted with sound otherwise your breath would not exist   not trying to be an asshole he offered   just sort of almost poetic

like most people/assholes I responded   I am concerned with sound when it suits me   I am an asshole he wrote

breath is labor I replied   naw he said breath is your every movement of language   poets do move language

he added   if you disagree then you're a prose writer! he laughed   maybe I said   I am feeling breath as labor

as in the work of giving birth   the movement of that work changed me   changed my poetry   movement

of sound   I like that he wrote back   I typed the word *meanwhile*   sent a photo from the morning paper

We Need a New Language of War it read   how could you give birth to sound? he said   not trying

to challenge he added   but do you think we exist because of sound?   waves and molecules I typed

make sound and light and matter   their sounds their friction cause existence   you mentioned labor

as breath he said   yes I wrote back   when French women say *oui* I said   they suck in a small breath

it sounds like the tiniest of blows   dang he wrote   I need some sleep!   good I said sleep   moon emoji send

MINORITY REPORT

"That's *my* break-up scene"   the poet wrote   and everything turned

to a near-perfect confection   of confession and universal feeling

he was Irish   or was he?   does it matter
                                      that in a movie I saw

a group of young Irish men   having been treated badly by England

liken themselves to Black Americans   does it matter
                                        that I was skeptical

of this comparison   despite my love of *The Dubliners*   my longing

to see a thousand shades of green
                              everything is relative these days

but still I try   to find meaning

meaning   if I was my children's first friend

then I hope one day   they'll be my friends again   meaning if love

is a dog from hell   then trust is her rescued cousin
                                  the other day

I heard the term *conspirituality*   which refers to the trend of luring people

towards conspiracy theories   on the internet   with the pretense

of spiritual practice   *Aha* I remarked   herein lies the history of man

too often and every day   I am thinking about words   like wind

my thoughts lift   and carry themselves away
                              how the ephemeral

is not soft but sharp   when it comes to pangs   a notion of mine

that now lives among the trees
                                    part of this   a friend tells me

is about not being ready internally   to reveal what the poem is about

Oh, you with your crystalline vision I say   *Tell me about the other parts*

CONSPIRACY THEORIES

My youngest son's   first word was *light*

No problem   his first expression

I was seven months pregnant with him   when my father died

my dad   who stumbled through life   improbably kind

I like to think he and my son   passed each other in the ether

of their creation and demise   that the universe conspired

to give me a buddha   at a time when I felt most alone

ten years later now   I'm reading about a mall

called *American Dream*   in East Rutherford, New Jersey

where you can stare   shopping straight in the face   if you dare

where every mirrored surface   is a gut punch to the conscience

and you can dry your hands   in a *Dyson* air blade without

looking up   or hurting any trees   everything

involves conspiracies   it seems

once I was texting my youngest son

How are you, hon? I asked

Good he wrote back   *When we were*
in Narragansett   we saw a rainbow cloud .

I'll show you a picture of it
and we saw a Nazi and a Ferrari

Wow I said   my actual face
 a laughing with horror emoji

Well I offered
It's Pride Day   so maybe

the cloud was God's way
of telling the Nazi off

Except God's not real   my son later said
He's a story   about a made-up friend

STABLE GENIUS OF LOVE

I'm no stable genius of love   but here I am

in heaven!
                I'm a fan of this

new dimension   where everyone would rather

believe women   than embrace   the knowledge monopoly

and I don't even need   to sleep to dream

                                        from on high
I can see the difference   between

privacy and surveillance   piracy and love

and I can spot   an actual dove   carrying

an olive branch   in her beak
                            so often

mistaken for a drone   flying alone

above the fray
                she charts a halo

around the Earth   a beacon

for stable geniuses   everywhere

steadily she goes

YOLO

Fear is stupid, so are regrets.
       —Marilyn Monroe

I.

Catherine says a tree out loud in your head matters

I know exactly what she means I've been listening to leaves

for a while now

      recently I read that Sylvia Plath

got an avocado for her 14th birthday it was her favorite gift

though even then she feared she was growing

decrepit at the same age my daughter is today

II.

I think about the way my kids laughed when I told them that

Laura Ingalls Wilder and her sisters were thrilled to find

oranges in their stockings at Christmastime

          a different world

I explained all rarity having been expunged from this one

the invisible obvious being

       what if dreams don't come true?

III.

A unit of meaning   me and you

also matters meaning   breathing into breathing

a lifetime   matters me   on paper acting

as if   this be that   be named my truth

until it be   an avocado   easily bruised

as girls
            but only some of them

IV.

Catherine also says   *patterns*
                       that poems are like math

or science   it's true when I'm in them   invisible natures align

and I sense systems
                as each morning

some American man   masturbating to Instagram   goes on

living his *best life*   straight-up with a fresh cup of YOLO

and the paper   saying it's a free country   is one way

his body summons   management of a place   that makes

him feel alone
             if we carried poems

instead of phones   what would come of it?

V.

My kids insist   the male version of Karen

should be Brad   making me wonder

at whose pleasure   he would serve   and if everyone

deserves a service creature   like that peacock

in business class   taking up three seats

its iridescent wings   clipped and blocking the aisle

VI.

This morning I told my youngest son   *Yes*

Google can be wrong   because people made Google

and people can be...
                          Boring is what he's thinking

so instead he tells me   that *Chicken Nug Life*   is his friend's

handle on *Fortnite*   Friend? I ask using air quotes   *Yes* he smiles

air quoting me back   we're laughing so hard about *nug*   I am doubled over

like the woman in the drawing   Terrance sent   the day of the coup attempt

a warding off he called it   prescient I said
                                        It's pretty funny my son gasps

Yes, honey I cry   *You have no idea   just how funny it is*

RICE

When I rinse the rice   I hear the word

Tamir   in the deepest part of my ear   how my mind

works at times   a not-so-free association   words

tethered to words   inexorably   a small part

of the heart broken
                              off and lodged   where language

fuses sound to meaning
                       Tamir

water running over rice

Tamir   meaning *He who walks tall*   ancient

purveyor of dates   sweet fruit of palm
                              Tamir

the rustle of his winter coat   against his labored

breath
       Tamir

RAGE AND IBUPROFEN

I know little   about matters   of practical application

it was being a waitress   that taught me   how to get along

that people want their food   and want it now   like everyone

my mind has regions
                            one for meat   one for bread

one for caravans   and tender age   one for rage

and ibuprofen
                    plus a whole zone for listening

past the migraines   to the dog whistles in the air   faint toll

of cowards ringing across time   history has to start somewhere

so, why not here?   I ask
                            my class to write

a letter to Mr. Baldwin   *because time catches up*

with kingdoms and crushes   also because I miss him

one girl writes:

> *Dear James,*
> *The most courageous thing*
> *a person can be is a Black woman.*

Damn, son   says the boy   at the desk behind her

and we all sit in silence   until the bell rings

STONE OF MY EXPERIENCE

At some point   Bonnie and Clyde came into it   I was young

knee-deep in love   seeking to soften my edges   but no matter

the hard truth   is that when the world   is breaking apart

one must get down
                    with the buddha

of one's innermost self   and ask what is work

and why one should do it
                    Mary advised me

to put the small   stone of my experience   on a personal altar

of sorts   so I can pick it up   from time to time   and remember

Diane said
            to shove at the thing   from all sides

and revolutionize   but it takes time   to get to the heart

of a matter
                at a crossroads   I thought

I'd like to photograph stones   then throw the photos

into the air   in the direction of the sun   a gesture towards

metaphor   but that now sounds   as baseless
                                    as Orlando

confessed he felt   the other day   when he spoke of his remorse

of men and their colonial ways
                              in America

we use words like   *profit*   *comfort*   *real estate*

as if they mean love   as if something   beyond utterance

has begun   just by saying them   but language is dumb

as any of us   it's a wonder   we work at all

ESSAY ON BEAUTY OR BEHOLD A TRUE STORY

There once was a man   who claimed   he couldn't watch *Bonnie and Clyde*

because Faye Dunaway   was too beautiful   it's true   beauty hurts

but it's seldom debilitating   overrated maybe   the way Meryl Streep

is *overrated*   in the eyes of a man   who doesn't find her beautiful enough

Fuck the bread
                    a writer's mother once said   when her daughter couldn't find

a teaching job   or yeast during a pandemic   *The bread* is over she told her

dismissing life   as we knew it   in one fell swoop
                                                    bread became language

to my mind   no longer elastic in form   all leavening lost

as bread became love   to my heart   a knot of kneading and need
                                                    another true story

is that I am a mother   and a writer   who knows about beauty and bread

about language and interruption   I also know the mirror only tells   part of the story

of a face   *The eyes have it*   they say   but the eyes can only hold so much

the way a heart can be full   and at the same time broken   different chambers

of a single system split
                    the way Faye Dunaway kills beauty

by being the mother of it   how we break bread   to partake of it

(WO)MANSPLAINING

After I gave birth
　　　　　　　　　to my first son　　my husband said something like

Why isn't everybody　　always talking about this?　　I mean, what else

is there to talk about?　　that is one way I came to understand　　why some

people talk all the time　　why some people speak very little
　　　　　　　　　　　　　　　　　　　　　　having babies

is also how I learned　　that the moment before anger　　is a moment

of need　　I carry life with me　　wherever I go

and whenever I speak　　I am talking about death

AT THE JETTY

Water breaking over the jetty   is water saying

fight if you must   is the moon conversing with the sea

advice for life   or advice in the case of an active shooter

sanctuary   were I a gun   sanctuary   even at sea

I'd love an emergency   as much as any tyrant

loves a crisis
                              better now to accept

that my phone is an asshole   that my life has grown

monstrous with ease   when the butcher told me

not to *overthink the meat*   on Christmas Eve

I didn't think too hard   about the cut or the mess

of presents beneath the tree   about presence or transcendence

I did reflect on *Paradise* though   that town reduced to ash

that crews spent days   sifting for remains   for pain

in its most granular form
                                        how every passion holds

clues to our vitality   network names like *Christ It's Loud*

or *Anxiety & Trauma*   spawn a thousand laugh emojis   including mine

as if   remind us we're alive   and we'll take it

every day is *not* the same   but related or referred

like pain or giant babies   we plod the earth   hacking our way

towards freedom   things that must be answered for
                                        Orlando says

in Navajo a computer is called   *metal that thinks*   which gets to the root

of it for me   how *placebo*   means *I please you*   how at my laptop sometimes

tears seep down into the motherboard   to the mother lode   to the whole mother

holding up half the sky
                        speak the names of those who were lost   please

not the names of those who took them   America is my home   please

but not my metaphor   not my body   as an expression of dirt

the margins of terror grow slim
                        and I survive

on an amazement of women   secret transactions   and the rage

of all the maidens at once
                        lodestar   bulwark   subtlety of fools

Opera is the music   in a movie of silence   my son declares

as I buckle him in   if you put that in a bottle   I swear I say

I will buy it
            I will rest my case

PERSONAL THEORY

It's like I'm deaf   and the letters are sounds

I can't see or read   with any accuracy   or maybe I'm blind

to signs   whose authority I give   too much weight

like trees   with their bark   all up in my face

tempting me   to mistake the forest   for peace

I've been meaning
                    to write Mary

about her lecture on evolution   and the brain

to say that
                once upon a time

I was on a date   when the young man said

I like your face   but while you're speaking   I keep seeing

your brain   it might have been   the best compliment

of my life   there was a second date   but not a third

it turned out   there was another girl
                                        but if we

had seen each other again   I would have told him

what I know about physics   and my personal theory

that the universe is a pact   sealed by faith   how gravity

leaks out   through cracks in space
                                which is what

makes gravity   the weakest force   and why we hold tight

to life   whether we like it or not   how otherwise

we'd float up   high above the trees   and have to claw

our way back   through the branches and leaves

be doomed to grasping   for roots to find footing

                        the illusion of solid ground

EMOTIONAL RESCUE

Is there nothing I can do   but be *steadfast and true*   eat trail mix every day

at 4:30 like Leah Umansky   who's on a strict *quarantine meal schedule*

which includes *panic snacks w/news*   and *dinner w/weird vibes*   I can't

be outside today   in the woods behind my house   because it's raining

and I'm feeling   too candy-ass   to put on boots
                                                          so here I sit

grieving on the couch   looking for faces   in the wood beams

on the ceiling   fear seems less   like a silent partner by my side   than a bolster

between me and my real guy   our real kids   who learned nothing at a *distance*

all week   because computers are lonely   and that's not how learning

works
         it hurts to see

how happy   my youngest son becomes   when his friend's face

shows up on Skype   like this is his new fun life   our new normal

each day's dreams   *like the night*   *dissolve off in sleep*   *promises*   *never meant to keep*

ESSAY ON MERCY

It's all management before mercy   for the suits at the rallies   and for those

alone in the ICU   not a single mask to reuse   even for the mothers

grieving in advance is intense   an anguish akin to combat   which it's said

feels like   the second before a car wreck   only all the time

                                                                        a single

prescient moment   right before impact   that tenses the body for eternity

bruises the psyche   and rewrites the system   to run solely on adrenaline

but mourning is not war

                                    and Antigone was not her brother

she sought to bury Polynices   because ritual is everything

so a warrior she became   still mythology continues

to bewilder   as if life doesn't train us   for death

it all remains grim   if we don't see   small mercies in our midst

the lessons we might miss   et cetera

                                        once when I was young

kissing a boy I didn't love   on a mattress in a floor-through

off 10th Avenue   I had the feeling   I was falling through time

it was then   only then   that life wasn't about saving things

                                       at least not mine

MIXED MOTIVE SITUATION

America really is   a mixed motive situation

between buffalo wings and yoga   it's confusing

I sent my hand-written question   to the desk seeking

clarification   on burden-sharing and absolute immunity

One nation under God   was the response I got

God's an imaginary friend I said   I reject him out-of-hand

You've waived your privilege   they replied   with that blanket

defiance you pretend   keeps you warm at night   *Get a man*

they intoned *Seek counsel*   but I acted as my own defense

self-representation was *excessive* they said   *No wonder you're not a 10*

DON'T PUSH ME WHEN I'M HOT

A lot of people won't get no supper tonight

 so I won't editorialize my burdens   except to say   that when we're talking about cake

we're using food as a substitute   the oldest recipe in the book   for what ails the heart

and mind
                   at times I find instant noodles   can serve as metaphor

for certain kinds of love   something about quick and cheap   or just add water

and wait
                   but phrases like *the end of days*   are not in my official read-out

I confess   every day is endless   shortcuts are conditional   that I also love my life

Laughing is one way
                   to say I hear you   or another form of sweetly talking trash

but my heart is multilingual   so you decide
                                      I'm busy memorializing my concerns

quick like the definition   you'd find in a dictionary of life   if you looked under *me and you*

Who am I to believe in dreams?   asked the great Anne Sexton   a different question

than the one   from that poet on the internet   who sub-tweeted her divorce

for all to see   a supposed proponent of *productive dreaming*
                                      but you be the judge

all I know is the Russians   are bombing Syrian villages   and calling it

Sending Candy   that *a Big Reveal*   can be about a kitchen   the make-up on a woman   or the highest office in the land

                                              that once upon a time

there lived a King   who admitted to his wife   that he wept upon meeting

the parents of children buried alive   in a mining accident, 1966

the Queen had to think   to ask her husband   if he had cried

unaccustomed as she was   to open displays of emotion

                                              maybe that's love

maybe it's not   *just remember to kick it over*   and *don't push me when I'm hot*

BREAKFAST OF CHAMPIONS

I woke up in a panic   this morning thinking   what if my *love language*

is granola?   I found a quiz online   but was too chicken to take it   having had

Russian bots once read   my face and place me   alongside a woman   holding a mango

or some bullshit in Gaugin
                          nothing *exotic* for me   today

for breakfast I'll take   a reflection on absurdity   short order/whiskey down

something like redemption   offered by a father   whose vanished mind failed

to recognize his own son   at the wheel of their car   how the father's approving nod

freed the son from
                          whatever   forgiveness

goes both ways   let's just say   I've discovered I know   how to hold a grudge

call me brittle   call me nuts even   but wouldn't you rather   call me *honey*

or sweetness in the morning   the giving the giving   the words the words

what if my one and only love   is language itself   lonely prospect   but O

affirmation   sweet breakfast of champions   grab a spoon and eat me up

NOTES

p. 16, "Essay on Gentrification" is for Tongo Eisen-Martin.

p. 18, "Treatise on My Mouth" is for Fiona Hill and borrows phrases from Hill's Opening Statement before the House Intelligence Committee Impeachment Inquiry of Donald Trump, November 21, 2019.

p. 22, My line "I can only be myself when my household is asleep" is a variation on a line in the poem "A Triste Little Tryst w/ R Frost, select billets-doux" by Jennifer Sperry Steinorth in her book, *A Wake with Nine Shades* (Texas Review Press, 2019).

p. 23, "Blue" borrows the phrase *focused immediacy* from "What I Miss Most About Swimming" by Bonnie Tsui, *New York Times,* April 10, 2020. It alludes to the phrase *blue mind,* coined by Wallace J. Nicolas, which is a state of mind in which discovery is fostered by being around water.

p. 29, It was the writer Paul Géraldy who first said "Memory is a poet, not an historian."

p. 31, "Hold" is for Nicole Callihan.

p. 33, "Joy in Repetition" is for Matthew Lippman.

p. 35 "green lucid" is a phrase Sylvia Plath writes in a letter that appears in *Red Comet* by Heather Clark.

p. 41, My line "Pray here. You can ask for anything" is me mis-hearing Carolyn Forché's line, "Pray here. You can ask for happiness" from her poem "Hue: A Notebook," from *In the Lateness of the World* (Penguin Press, 2020), which she read virtually "in" Dublin during the early part of the pandemic.

p. 49, In "Essay on Movement" the writer I reference is Leslie Jamison, and her piece "Since I Became Symptomatic," which appeared in *The New York Review* on March 26, 2020.

p. 51, "Going Through Some Things": The title here is a reference to Donald Trump's veiled threat against former United States Ambassador to Ukraine, Marie Yovanovitch. Trump told Ukrainian president Volodymyr Zelensky, "She is going to go through some things."

p. 53, "What We Talk About When We Talk About Paths: a Narrative in Captions" is composed of a year's worth of near-daily captions on my Instagram account, roughly March 2019-March 2020. The title is a riff on Raymond Carver's short story, "What We Talk About When We Talk About Love."

p. 64, The line "Without Bringing Any Other People into the Planning Loop / I Have Decided to Have Breakfast" is a variation borrowed from Mary Ruefle's poem, "The Good Fortune of Material Existence," from *Dunce*, Wave Books, 2019.

p .75, In "Libretto," the poem/poet I refer to is "For You" by Sharon Olds, which first appeared in *The New Yorker* on May 14, 2018.

p. 84, "Minority Report" is for Terrence Degnan, and borrows the phrase "That's my break-up scene" from his poem, "This is My Beach."

p. 88, "Stable Genius of Love": The title of this poem refers to Donald Trump's assertion that he is a *stable genius*. It is also a riff on the song "Genius of Love" by Tom Tom Club, on their album of that name, released by Compass Point Studios, Nassau, Bahamas, 1981.

p. 92, "Rice" was composed as part of a collaboration with the One Gun Gone, anti-violence project based in Providence, Rhode Island.

p. 93, "Rage and Ibuprofen": *my mind has regions* is a phrase borrowed from James Baldwin's essay "Letter from a Region in My Mind," which appeard in *The New Yorker*, 1962.

p. 94, "Diane" is Diane di Prima. "Mary" is Mary Ruefle.

p. 98, "At the Jetty": *monstrous with ease* is a phrase borrowed from Kaveh Akbar's poem, "The Place," which I heard him read at AWP 2019, in Portland, Oregon.

p. 102, "Emotional Rescue": The title of this poem is borrowed from the Rolling Stones' song of the same name, as are the lines, *Is there nothing I can do (but) be steadfast and true and like the night (eventually) dissolve off in sleep, promises (were) never meant to keep.*

p. 105, In "Don't Push Me When I'm Hot," the line *A lot of people won't get no supper tonight* comes from the song, "Armagideon Time" by The Clash, on *Black Market Clash*, Epic Records, 1980.

ACKNOWLEDGMENTS

Grateful for previous publication of the following poems:

p. 13, "Year of the Murder Hornet" appears on poets.org

p. 16, "Essay on Gentrification" first appeared on Tribes.org, August 2021.

p. 17, "Essay on Poetics or Early Morning Texting with Orlando" was published in *The Literary Review*, Winter 2020.

p. 18, "Treatise on My Mouth" is included in *Stronger Than Fear: Poems of Empowerment, Compassion, and Social Justice*, Ed. by Carol Alexander and Stephen Massimilla, Cave Moon Press, 2021.

p. 20, "Shelter in Place" appeared in *Love's Executive Order*, March 20, 2020.

p. 26, "Designated New Yorker," was featured on *Rhode Island Weekly*, Sept 7, 2021, Rhode Island Public Television, for the 20th anniversary of Sept. 11.

p. 28, "Regime" was published by *The Common*, Poetry Feature, August 2021.

p. 30, "Disposable Mask": an earlier version of this poem appears in the anthology *Processing Crisis*, Risk Press and St. Mary's College of California, 2022.

p. 31, "Hold" appears in *Mom Egg Review*, March 2021.

p. 34, "Ideas" appears in *Soul Lit*, Fall 2021.

p. 41, "Come Correct" appears in *Mom Egg Review*, March 2021.

p. 44, "Poem by a Person Called a Woman" appears in *Love's Executive Order*, October 19, 2018.

p. 50, "Essay on States" was published by *The Common*, Poetry Feature, August 2021.

p. 53, Excerpts from "What We Talk About When We Talk About Paths" were published in *The Literary Review*, Winter 2020

p. 80, "Mysterious Ways" appears in *Soul Lit*, Fall 2021.

p. 84, "Minority Report" first appeared on Tribes.org, August 2021.

p. 89, "Yolo" appears in the anthology *I Want to Be Loved by You: Poems on Marilyn Monroe*, Milk & Cake Press, 2022.

p. 93, "Rage and Ibuprofen" was published by the on-line journal *Action Spectacle*, Spring 2020.

p. 96, "Essay on Beauty or Behold a True Story" appears in *Love's Executive Order*, October 4, 2020.

p. 98, "At the Jetty" was published by the on-line journal *Action Spectacle*, Spring 2020.

p. 107, "Breakfast of Champions" was published by *The Common*, Spring 2022.

SHOUT-OUTS

Deep gratitude to my family and friends for love and support; to my son, Cormac, for use of his photo for my cover; to Sean Singer for crystalline (re)vision and encouragement; to Matthew Lippman for being a mensch; to Michael Morse for years of friendship; to a veteran in the truest sense: Colin Channer; to John Hennessy—always supportive and kind; to Greg Pardlo for ongoing generosity; to Camille Guthrie for diamond-like brilliance and inspiration; to Mary Ruefle for her wit and wisdom; to Orlando White for late-night ruinations; to Sheila Maldonado and Matthew Zapruder and Sandra Simonds and Natalie Schapiro and Terence Degnan and Nicole Hefner Callihan and Tongo Eisen-Martin and all the poets everywhere for vibes and inspiration. As always, eternal thanks to Laura Cesarco Eglin and Veliz Books for their continued support and belief in my work.